The Way We Were

Roni Jenkins and Selena Jenkins

authorHOUSE®

AuthorHouse™ UK Ltd.
500 Avebury Boulevard
Central Milton Keynes, MK9 2BE
www.authorhouse.co.uk
Phone: 08001974150

First published by AuthorHouse 11/16/2009

ISBN: 978-1-4490-4666-8 (sc)

This book is printed on acid-free paper.

Contents

Chapter 1

I was born in Jamaica to parents called Raymond and Ethel who I thought loved me. I am one of eight children; there are five boys and two girls starting with the eldest, Patrick, Patty, Melvin, Kingston, me, Jane, John and Paul and have a British Nationality.

The house where we were living was not very big, we had two bedrooms; all the children were sleeping in one room and our parents in the other. We had wooden floors throughout the house, the kitchen was different from the ones over here, and it was separated from the house, in another building where the cooking was done on a coal fire and a dining table. The toilet was separated in its own building with two very deep holes accompanied with lids, a big and small one, which was also wooden.

The house was at the front of the yard with the kitchen and toilet at the back but both distant from each other. We had some fruit trees in the yard, there were two big fruit trees at the back, two more at the front a lime tree on one side and a grapefruit on the other side in the front yard in total we had six fruit trees.

The house did not have a living room, as we know it; instead, we had a veranda where people would sit when they came around. We had a pig, a cat, cows, goats, dogs and chickens. My cat was stolen and my pig died. We did not have a television so as children we had to entertain our selves we had many games to keep us busy.

When I started school, I was around five or six years old and I had to walk approximately two miles away from home by myself. There was only one school that I knew of in the district where everyone attended. I went to the same school as my aunts and uncles who were in the year above me, except for one of my uncles who was in the same year. I remember when I was a little girl, I was afraid of the dark and as a child, not having a lot of space, I accidentally broke my mother's china plates. She heard and in the dark she pushed me outside trying to lock me out. I cried and begged her not to but being the callous woman that she is, she did it anyway. I should have known then what my life would have turned out to be.

My father Raymond, who I did not know at the time, was living in England. My mother Ethel also came over to England leaving us children behind on our own until they decided to bring us over.

Chapter 2

I was nine years old when we came to England my younger brother Paul was already over here because he came with my mother when he was a baby, the rest of us came over together, it was on the 9th of September 1966 when we arrived (it was the that my life in Jamaica had ended). I remember wearing a blue dress with a blue rose on each side. Our very first home was in East Ham it was a three bedroom house which accommodated ten people, Patty,

Jane and I would share the smallest room, our brothers Patrick, Melvin, Kingston, John and Paul would share the largest.

Due to not having a lot of contact with Raymond when I was living in Jamaica, it resulted in me not knowing him so when I first came I would not talk to Raymond, I was afraid of him. Once Raymond spoke to me and I cried. As time went by I got use to him, Ethel and Raymond on the other hand would argue so much, more than normal to the point where we as kids would hear everything that they were saying. When I was in Jamaica, I was very close to my siblings it was not until we immigrated to England when things started to change. I became very quiet and isolated. I started Primary School, which was not too bad; I attended it with my younger sister Jane who is a year younger than me. As we got older, I started to notice a difference between my siblings and I and the way our mother treated us; suddenly I became the black sheep of the family.

One night, my mother sent Jane and I to the laundrette (this was a Sunday night) and because Ethel did not trust me with anything due to the fact that she believed I was incapable, that left Jane holding the money for the washing. After the laundrette we went home, Jane gave Ethel the change, Ethel put the money on the fridge so Jane took the 50p to buy sweets on the way to school the next day.

Even though we attended the same school Jane and I never had anything to do with one another, in fact we really did not speak to each other because we had our own circle of friends. When Ethel found out the 50p went missing, she called both Jane and myself and asked for the money, I told her that I did not know where it was and Jane denied the whole thing. Ethel then said that she was going to search our belongings for the money and because Jane knew she had it, she asked if she could go upstairs and do something. When Jane went upstairs, she took the money from her clothes and put it under a stone where she could retrieve it in the morning on her way to school but things did not go quite as planned because she got caught and then trouble began.

Being the unfair and unfeeling woman that Ethel is, she accused me of taking the money even though I told her that I did not know anything about it which was the truth. Ethel did not believe me, she said...

"You took it so that you could buy sweets to share with Jane."

Despite the fact that the evidence was found in Jane's belongings, my mother beat me that night along with Jane even though she deserved it and I didn't.

My mother would always dress myself and Jane in the same clothes but different colours sometimes, I remember a jumper that we both use to have, nothing was different about the two except that Jane rolled her sleeves up and I didn't. On one particular day, I was told to put the clothes in the washing machine which I did, I put Jane's jumper in along with my own, her jumper stilled rolled up so that we knew the difference, when the clothes came out of the machine, Jane's jumper had stretched therefore it was no good to her but she wanted mine. I had to fight just to keep my own jumper but it was of no use because when Ethel heard what was going on, she gave my jumper to Jane. I was so furious but because I had no one to stand up for me, I kept quiet, this did not help the relationship between Jane and I, we fought every morning, every opportunity we had, we would fight. I could not stand her at all;

as far as I was concerned my would always take her side over mine and so I became more and more withdrawn, it did not help with the constant arguing between Raymond and Ethel.

Paul, Melvin, Kingston, Patty, Jane, John and I, were not allowed to go into the living room where Ethel had the sofa and the telephone (which she also put a lock on). When she cleaned the room, we were forbidden to go in there. We couldn't, even if we tried because Ethel would lock the door.

We could not eat anything without asking her first. One day, Ethel made a cake and told us not to touch it but Patrick, the eldest of the siblings ad cut the cake and eaten it, which no one else knew about. Ethel saw it and called Jane, John, Paul and myself (the four younger ones) and asked us which one had cut the cake and eaten it, we all denied doing it but she did not believe and so her answer to us was...

"The four older ones would not lie therefore it has to be one of the four younger ones."

After hearing this, I believed that it was her way of trying to single me out again, and so that night the four of us was beaten badly for 'lying'. When Ethel had finished beating us, she took the cake and threw it away saying...

"If it is a ghost who came and ate the cake, then I do not want it," (she was over dramatizing a simple situation as usual) that was when Patrick had owned up to eating the cake but the four of us younger ones never got an apology for the beating and for being called a liar, Patrick was never punished for what he had done.

Because Patty, Jane and I had the smallest room, it was only a bunk bed that was able to fit in there. One night after Raymond and Ethel's famous argument she decided to sleep in our room, back then we used a gas heater which you had to adjust, but during the night the gas heater went out, spreading the fumes around the room, in the morning Raymond smelt the fumes and tried to wake us up, including Ethel but we did not respond, he then opened the windows and door to ventilate the room while constantly trying to get us up. Eventually, we opened our eyes and then left the room, during the day we had all developed headaches.

About three years later I was at the age of twelve, the house became smaller and smaller so Ethel went out looking for a bigger place, she found a five bedroom house which she put a down payment of £20 for the holding fee until they were able to pay the reasonable amount. I was looking forward to moving into the new house. Patty, Jane and I continued to share a room as well as Kingston, John and Paul meanwhile the two eldest ones had a room of their own. By the time I was a year into my secondary school, I had lost all my confidence due to the fact that I was fat (not to the point where I was obese) and all the other kids were teasing me, they would call me names and say things like...

"Nigger, go back to your country and go swing on your banana tree."

Because of the constant name calling from the other kids at school, fighting with Jane on a daily basis and the never ending feud between Ethel and Raymond, I became even more withdrawn. I was finally taken out of secondary school and transferred to another one where I was put into the lowest classes. When I passed my exams, my own mother did not believe me until she saw my results.

I must have been so withdrawn for Ethel to notice, she thought that I was crazy saying that she was worried about me, thinking that it was madness, she took me to see a psychiatrist who after tested me said that there was nothing wrong with me. After hearing what the psychiatrist said, Ethel disrupted my education by taking me out the school I was attending to put me into a school for children with learning disabilities. I attended that school for a few months where I had the teachers telling my mother that I was too bright for that school so she took me out.

All this time Raymond stood by and did absolutely nothing to help me, he did not care what happened to me. After being uprooted again from different schools, I was fifteen years old when I attended an all girls' school which for me was not a pleasant experience because I had to endure suffering from my head of year who was extremely racist.

We had a park nearby where all the boys would go and bother all the girls but because I was very shy, I would make sure I took another route home. Anyway, one day while I was at school, my head of year made a comment which surprised me. She said…

"If it was down to me, I would kick all the black kids out of my school" and because she had that kind of mind, she decided to make trouble for me by telling my mother that I would skip school and go to the park with the boys, which was not true. But as usual, Ethel believed someone else over me, even though I told her that my head of year was a racist because of the comment that she made about all the black kids in my school, and that she was trying to cause trouble for me by making up that lie. I should have kept my mouth shut, because Ethel's words to me were…

"No teacher would say that."

I knew that no matter what I did, I could never win when it came to my relatives and other people I always came at the bottom against everyone else, the sad thing is, I never lied to her.

Then I finished school.

Chapter 3

I was at the age of sixteen when I had finished school and started working in a factory where they sewed money bags for the banks. I worked from 08:00 to 5:00 everyday.

I came on my cycle (I had started my period at the age of twelve) and because Ethel had not told me about becoming a woman, and what happens. I did not know how to tell her, and even if I did, I could not because we did not have that kind of mother daughter relationship. I remember using toilet paper for pads but it was of no use because I would bleed right through my dress or whatever I was wearing that day. One Sunday, I was on my period and the blood had gone through my dress (as usual), Ethel saw and sent one of my brothers to tell me that she wanted to talk to me. When I got to my parents bedroom, she told Raymond to beat me, and while he was beating me, Ethel so kindly informed me that all women get that.

Because I was a heavy bleeder I remember another time when I came on, I had bled right through my skirt, I took my skirt off and put it to soak in the

water along with everything else that I was wearing, Ethel took one look at my skirt and said the most nastiest thing that I will never forget, she said...

"It looks like you have been raped."

The name calling in the house, which was always directed at me, was a constant thing. One day Jane called me a fat slub so I hit her, it escalated into a massive fight, which Ethel had to get involved in, taking Jane's side by telling me to apologise to her. I tried to explain to Ethel about what Jane called me, but I never got my apology because Ethel just did not care about me enough to be fair so I still got in trouble.

Melvin and Kingston went away to university; Patrick was sleeping with an older woman around the same time she got pregnant. She decided to blame the pregnancy on him by telling Patrick that he was the father of her unborn child, after hearing this, Patrick decided to marry her which meant that he had to leave home, leaving the rest of us feeling scared of Ethel because of her controlling and callous nature. It did not last very long because at the age of seventeen, Jane also became pregnant Patty was the only one who knew about her pregnancy.

One day, Jane decided to tell Ethel about the baby that she was carrying, (I found out the same time Ethel did) Ethel argued with Jane about it for a while and then decided to accept it because Jane stayed at home until her baby daughter was born.

So John, Paul and I were still living at home, Kingston and Melvin was still attending two different universities. Patrick however, was at the age of twenty two, married with a daughter and a home of his own, Jane had her baby at the age of eighteen and then left home, she also got her own flat. Even though Jane was really nasty to me when we were younger, I decided to put that aside and help her out with the baby so I put a deposit on a cot for her daughter. When Ethel asked Jane about the baby's father she told her that it was someone from school, it was not much to be proud of because the guy she was seeing did not like Jane very much because when Jane had told him about her pregnancy his response to that was...

"Out of all the women in the world look who I got stuck with."

Patty was also seeing a guy which Ethel had no idea about, because their relationship was not too either even though Ethel hated me, Patty and Ethel used to butt heads a lot until one night I was down stairs when Patty called to me, when I got to her bedroom, I was shocked at what I saw, there on the bed along with Patty were pills that she had intended to swallow just so she could end her life, I was scared because it had hit me what Patty would have done, I did not want her to kill herself so I took the pills and flushed them down the toilet.

It was a nightmare living in that house Ethel wore the pants in the family no one could and would dare to say anything to her for fear of upsetting her knowing that she was an abusive woman. After that night when Patty attempted suicide, she started to go out more and in doing so, she became pregnant which meant that she had to marry the father of her baby because our mother would not allow unwed mothers in our family, while Patty was planning her wedding, she got cold feet and decided to opt out of the wedding,

I had to talk to her so that she could see the reason for her to continue with the wedding this is what I said to her...

"You are afraid and because of that, you are getting cold feet, I know that you love him and he loves you," and her reply was...

"Yes that is true," so I continued by saying...

"There is no reason why you should not go through with this marriage." So after the conversation, Patty ended up going through with the wedding and that meant she too left home.

Altogether, it was Kingston, Patrick, Patty, Melvin and Jane who were no longer living at home. The relationship between Ethel and myself had not improved at all, Raymond and I never bonded as father and daughter in fact we never really communicated but every time Ethel would have one of her turns, Raymond would stay out of the way and do absolutely nothing to help me.

By this time, I was no longer working at the factory but in the West End coming home and then off to college while Ethel would work shifts, come home around 3:00 in the afternoon and sit around the house doing nothing all day, she refused to iron her and Raymond's clothes, she would not clean the house, wash the dishes or go shopping, me on the other hand would come home from work which started from 09:00 to 5:00, cook the dinner, clean the house, put the clothes in the washing machine, take them out and hang them out to dry and then iron every single one of the clothes before I headed off to college in the evenings, so I was incredibly tired. I would also go shopping on Saturdays.

No matter how much chores I had Ethel was never satisfied, she always had problems with what I did and the way I did them, it did not help because I was the only girl still living at home. One day Ethel said to me...

"Because you are the only girl left, I expect you to pull my skirt down" (whatever that meant).

Ethel was extremely abusive to me, she was physically, mentally and verbally abusive towards me, she would always play mind games, which she was very good at, very manipulative, she had ways of hurting you and then making you feel as though you are the one who treated her badly, being around her made me feel suicidal and this was on a daily basis, she would say really nasty and hurtful things to me such as...

"You are a worthless trash, a worthless good for nothing, you are dead but your two eyes are open, you are breathing the breath that someone else should have, you will never amount to anything in life and that no man would want you."

These are the comments that I would hear from my own mother everyday of my life in that house, sometimes I would get a break when I was not at home but it would not last for very long because on one occasion, I remember after Patty got married and had her baby she invited me to her home and because Ethel and Patty were not seeing eye to eye, she asked me to bring

Paul, knowing that I could not just bring Paul, I had to ask Ethel first and her response to me was...

"I do not want Paul going with you to Patty's because I do not want anything to happen to him."

I could not understand where she was coming from because as far as Patty and I were concerned, Paul was our baby brother and we would not let

anything happen to him but I could not argue with Ethel so I left it at that. When I arrived at Patty's house, she asked for Paul, I told her what Ethel had said to me needless to say that Patty was not very happy so she mentioned it to Patrick who then decided to call a family meeting (a start of many), Ethel's comments concerning Paul came out but she denied everything which did not surprise me. But she turned to me and called me a house murderer for telling Patty what she said; she also said that she was going to the grave with me in her heart.

The slander continued and adding to that, she said to me...

"If I were your brothers and sisters, I would not let anyone know that you are my sister," and how I poisoned her children's minds against her. Ethel had a very bad habit of talking about me behind my back, she would always talk about me to the boys and girls saying nasty things about me, when Paul was old enough to understand she would bring him in on the act and when I used to hear what she said, it would hurt a lot, I would wonder how can a woman who call herself a mother be so cruel towards her own child.

At the time of the meeting, Ethel was making comments and telling a lot of lies until I could not take it any more, I snapped and the next thing I knew, I was running down the road in floods of tears Paul and Patty came after me, they said that they were not going to allow me to run like that because I could have easily run underneath a car considering the mental state that I was in. I took that chance to fill Paul in on what I told Patty about the things Ethel said to me concerning him and Paul confirmed that what I said was true, I asked him if I was lying about the whole thing and he said...

"No."

And that was the end of that conversation.

I was an emotional wreck at home that when I got to work I would be sitting there crying to myself everyday until one day one of my colleagues asked me if I was going to cry myself to death. I always dreaded the end of the day because I knew that I would be going home and I could not deal with that, home to me became such a bad place I did not know what to do, I hated it.

On one particular day, Melvin and Kingston came home from their universities to find Ethel having a go at me, it got to the point where I could not control myself, I was shaking so much that Melvin had to step in and he said to Ethel...

"Why can't you leave her alone? You are always picking on her."

Ethel was so furious at what Melvin had said she started shouting and behaving badly. No matter how hard I tried, I just couldn't deal with what was going on at home, I cried myself to sleep most nights and the other nights I could not sleep at all which was not good for me because I had to get up early in the morning.

Going to work, college and doing the housework on limited sleep was very painful for me but I was not allowed to complain, I had to pull myself together and continue with what I was doing. One day, Ethel put her clothes on the washing line to dry and when I came home from work I started washing the dishes before I headed off to college, Ethel ordered me to pick her clothes up off the washing line so I told her that I was washing up before I went off to college but it made no difference to her, her reply to me was...

"It is my clothes and you have to go and take them off the line because I will not be doing it."

Ethel had no respect for me as a person with feelings she talked about me to anyone who would listen even if I found out she would not care because I was hated so much by her and even until today, I do not know why.

"Maybe it was the sight of me that made her so mad," I thought.

One day, I was sweeping the kitchen floor, Ethel walked in, knocked me over and started to punch and kick me in the head, when she got like this, there was no stopping her. Raymond, who was in the house, did nothing to stop her.

It was so bad I had to ask Raymond if her behaviour towards me was my fault, and he never gave me an answer that helped me, he said...

"Whether or not" and that was it, he never supported me and so based on that, I apologised to her.

Of all the nasty things that a mother could say to a child, what Ethel said next was by far the sickest comment that could have ever left her mouth that day, because I really needed someone to talk to, I tried to ask my father various questions to try and understand why Ethel was behaving like this towards me alone and even though he was not very helpful Ethel said...

"You and your father must have a secret for each other," implying that something was going on between myself, and my own father. After that day Raymond went completely cold towards me and started treating me badly and then things got increasingly worse, at that point, I was truly alone.

Ethel has a gift of projecting her feelings onto someone else, is she hated you; she would go around telling people that you hated her, which is what she kept doing to me.

Raymond was now in the act, Ethel would talk about me to him and he wouldn't say a word to her. In my opinion he failed as a father, I did not know how to respect him as a father or a man because all I could see was a man who let his wife control everyone and everything, he never voiced his views as the man of the house (or suppose to be).

Half the time, I would forget that he was around because he never protected me from my mother. I had enough with everything so when I came home from wherever I went; I would go straight to my room so that I would stay out of Ethel's way. One evening, I came home, I went to my bedroom and started combing my hair, then all of a sudden my door burst wide open and there stood Ethel at the door having a go at me again, she told me that my hair was going to fall out amongst other rotten things that she said to me that night.

With everything that she was saying to me on a regular basis putting me down and constantly knocking my self-esteem, lowering my confidence at any given opportunity that she had, I started to believe that I was indeed a failure, pathetic not worth anything especially to be loved by anyone, I found it impossible to love myself.

Chapter 4

There was a well known store called Dickens & Jones where I used to work, I had a bank account which Raymond had access to. He had saved a lot more money than me even though I was unaware of how much he had actually saved. The £100 that I had saved, I asked him to credit it into my bank account on his way home from work, unaware that Raymond had kept my money instead of depositing it.

It was about three weeks later when I was in my room, my bedroom door burst wide open, Raymond came in and without saying a word he threw an envelope on my bed, by this time I was confused by his actions, he just stood there with his arms folded and when I opened the envelope I saw an electric bill for £100, I asked Raymond if he had put the money into my account and he said...

"No."

I told him that he could use my £100 to pay the bill, so he took the envelope and without so much as a thank you, he left and I never saw my £100 or heard anything from him concerning it again.

Raymond had a habit of borrowing money from me and not paying me back. On another occasion he asked me if I could lend him £5 which I did, a few weeks later I needed some money so I borrowed £5 from Raymond, he kept asking me for his money back, so I asked him...

"What about my £5."

And he said...

"It is dead money," (implying that I would not be getting my money back).

Even though I was already paying my rent there, the financial stress for me became greater because Ethel told me that I had to give her money when I started working because she helped me to get the job regardless of the fact that she was still working for her own money as well as Raymond, I still had to give her what I was earning.

Work was my safe haven and that was where I met Winston (because he came to work there too), we started talking and in due time he took an interest in me (or so I thought), we started seeing each other socially while things at home were getting progressively worse. Then one Christmas I was invited to a Christmas dinner with all my colleagues which I agreed to, I had to inform Ethel about this before. On the night that I went out, I rang home so that Ethel would not worry but it made no difference because when I got home, she went stark raving mad and started punching me in the head she would not stop even though I was blacking out, while this was happening, she kept saying to me that I was bringing shame and disgrace on her. I could not take it anymore so I walked out that night and went to stay with a colleague, Ethel did not care but Patrick went looking for me. My colleague (the one I was staying with) said to me that I should phone my family so I phoned Patrick and I went to stay with him and his wife, not knowing what Ethel would have said to him, he came home crying saying that Ethel had cursed him and telling Patrick that...

"If it had not been for you then Vanessa would come back home."

After hearing this, Patrick then told me that if I want to leave home, I cannot do it from his place so he took me back to Ethel's house a place where I could no longer call home because I felt so unsafe and unloved, it was more of a foreign place to be.

When I returned to the house, Ethel had called someone she knew to talk to me, she never said why I was behaving the way I did because she wanted to make it look like I was out of control. Ethel then turned around and said to me that I was no longer welcome to use her pots, pans, cutleries e.t.c, which made me feel even more like a stranger in my own home even though I felt this way, it did not bother me too much because I bought my own things and asked Patty to hold them for me until I got a place of my own which was a big mistake.

So I said to Ethel, Raymond and their friend that...

"If I am going to be a stranger, I'd rather be one outside of the house," and so I left and never went back.

Chapter 5

Ever since I can remember, Ethel and her husband never treated me decently, I never felt as though I was a part of the family, even my brothers and sisters had their turn of making me feel absolutely useless and for that I did not want anything else to do with them all so eventually I found a one room where I was staying, Winston asked his sister Maggie if she could help me out and she agreed.

One day, one of the girls from work told me that Winston was talking about me; I knew that he would not have said anything nice so I decided that I did not want anything to do with him also, so I never spoke to him, Winston, being a spoilt brat that he was, rang Maggie and told her that I was not talking to him and that I wanted nothing to do with him, Winston then told me that his sister wanted me to ring her which I did and it was on the phone when she said to me...

"You expect me to help you but you are not even talking to my brother."

I had no idea what else he said to his sister but she really laid it on thick as to why I should talk to her brother so because I needed her help, my situation drove me to get involved with him again.

I moved out of the one room flat and into Maggie's house and that was when I found out I was pregnant with my first child at the age of twenty four, I had no idea which one of the two Winston or Maggie who had spilled the beans concerning my whereabouts because Melvin and Patrick both came to see me which I was unhappy about. I moved out of Maggie's house and into Rosa, another one of Winston's sisters, I continued to work right through my pregnancy until it was time for me to give birth to my daughter. After my baby was born and I was still in hospital, Jane and Patrick came to visit me, they caused problems and left. I was at home for four months on maternity leave and while I was at home tending to my baby, Winston would come home very late at night I knew it was not work that was holding him up, I knew this because we worked at the same store and I was aware of what time the store closed.

Winston would leave home at 08:00 in the morning and he would not return home until 10:00 at night sometimes even later. While I was still living with Rosa, Winston said to me...

"You should take Tori (my baby) to go see Ethel."

I could not understand why he would suggest that to me because he knew before we started seeing each other that Ethel and I did not have a very good relationship which is why I wanted nothing else to do with her and her family, but even though I felt this way, against my better judgement, I went to see her anyway a trip that I was not looking forward to. When I got there, Ethel was upstairs and Raymond was in the kitchen, Jane and Melvin was also visiting them that day, Jane took Tori upstairs so Ethel could see her, they were upstairs for no longer than a second when Jane came back down, she told me that Ethel had turned her back on Tori and did not even look at my baby, so I went to say hello to Raymond and he too turned his back on me without an answer.

When I stood out in the hall way at the foot of the stairs, Ethel stood at the top of the stairs and started shouting verbal abuse at me, she said...

"You have come to show off your baby, I have eight of my own and they are Patrick, Patty, Melvin, Kingston, you Jane, John and Paul," even though she did not consider me as one of her children.

Ethel kept going on so I took my baby from Jane and walked out feeling hurt and sorrowful. As I was walking to the station, I did not realise that I had walked so fast so when Melvin came after me and caught up he asked me if I was running, I replied...

"No."

I went back to Rosa's house, knowing that Kingston was getting married I did not bother attending his wedding. My baby Tori and I were living in the basement; I would cook Winston's meals and keep it warm for him when he decided to come home, but more often than not, he would stay away I believed that he was cheating on me and because it was causing problems for me, I asked him to leave but he refused and even though my gut feeling told me that he was cheating on me, he denied the whole thing. One day, my work colleagues wanted to see Tori so I went to my work place with her and on my way back from the station I saw Winston with another woman, he had his arm around her waist laughing, they did not see us and I did not let him know that I saw him, I just watched. When he saw me, he was shocked, he disappeared with the woman that he was with for a while and them he returned, he uttered the famous quotation…

"It's not what it looks like I was just telling her a joke."

Like I believe that, he must have thought that I was born yesterday, so I went home with my baby. I realised that I could not trust this man, he had taken advantage of my vulnerability and hurt me in the most unforgivable way. When he came home early the next day, he was still trying to explain, but I did not want to hear any of it, I have always hated lying, especially when it is to my face and so after feeding me a lot of garbage Winston must have thought that I was stupid enough to believe what he said but that was not the case.

I used to get income support for Tori which came as a book, I would go to the post office and cash the money but on one occasion, I went to cash my money, just to find that my book was missing, I searched everywhere for it but could not find my book so I went to the post office to find out if it was handed in but the lady who worked there said…

"No."

The room that I was living in did not have a lock and key which meant that anyone could have walked in a taken my book along with my favourite pair of gold earrings. Searching frantically around my room, I decided to ask Rosa and her daughters if they had seen my book and gold earrings and their reply was…

"No we have not seen it."

So I decided to forget about the missing items because there was nothing that I could do about them so I went out as I would usually do and when I got back to my room, my income support book had mysteriously found it's way back on my bed with money withdrawn from it leaving my baby and I with nothing to live on for that time, I believed that it was Sandra, Rosa's daughter who stole them.

Chapter 6

Winston also has a brother called Oliver who we used to go and visit, as time went by I grew to distrust him as well based on the things that he used to do and say. Oliver would have me believe that he told Winston not to mess me around, but I knew that Oliver had ulterior motives, it was almost as if the minute people met me, they felt the need to gossip about me because Oliver would talk about me behind my back to his brother Winston (the father of my child), and both Winston and Oliver would talk about me to their niece Melinda the daughter of Jesse who is another brother of theirs.

Melinda also had a sister called Lucy who was nothing like them and wanted very little to do with her family because she knew how badly they behaved and so she kept her distance by going into hiding where the rest of the family were unable to find her. Winston would say things to Melinda about me, things like...

"Vanessa trapped me by getting pregnant," he conveniently forgot to mention that I did not want anything to do with him and it was between him and his sister Maggie why I ended up back with him. Long before I had my baby, I told him to go and get out of my life but he would not listen to me and now there he was making me out to be the bad guy in all of this. At that time, I had no idea that he was talking about me, but as this story progresses, I will tell you how I found out.

Winston has three brothers and two sisters, their names are Oliver, Leroy, Jesse, Maggie and Rosa. Winston would poison his brothers and sisters minds against me by telling them bad things which were untrue, he talked about me to Leroy and his wife Millie, but they were different Millie would report back to me what her brother told her. On one occasion Winston said something to her and her reply to him was...

"If Vanessa is so bad, why don't you leave her?" (A valid question, I thought) but he had no answer.

After my four months maternity leave, I went back to work so I had to find a child minder who was willing to look after my baby Tori, I eventually found one believing that she was good; I bought plenty of nappies and food for my baby so all she had to do was change and feed her, I realised that Tori's child minder was not looking after her at all, when I finished work I would pick Tori

up from her child minder's just to find my baby in her pushchair and when I got home to change her nappy, she would be soaking wet, raw and red with urine it was as if her child minder had not changed her all day, I felt like this woman was taking my money and not taking care of my baby.

So I decided to take care of Tori myself which meant that I was no longer able to work, it was a hard decision for me to make because I knew that I would be struggling financially and with no child support from her father, but I felt that I'd rather look after my baby myself than trust her in someone else's care, with my decision in motion, I continued working that same year and gave it up the following year to be a full time mother to Tori.

Myself and Tori finally moved out of the area that we were living in and moved into a two bedroom flat on the fourth floor, being afraid of heights, I was petrified to look out of the window let alone stay close to it which meant that cleaning would be a nightmare, I had to stand on a chair even though my knees and hands would go weak but I knew the job had to be done.

Living in a new borough, I was very glad because I knew that Ethel and her family would not find me there, trying to get away from them, I thought that life was finally peaceful but it did not last long because Winston knew where I was living, I felt so uneasy about that due to the fact that I knew he would have opened his big mouth and tell my so-called family, my suspicions were right , one night the door bell rang and to my shock and dismay, there stood Jane and Patty, I was fuming

"How did they know where to find me" I thought at that point I realised that no matter what I did and where I went, I could not seem to get away from them.

From that day onward, Ethel and her family wanted me to visit them it has always been like this, what Ethel wanted, Ethel gets no matter who she has to use to get it Raymond would never speak up about anything that went on in his life, he always let his wife control everything that happened, and that included him.

When Tori was around five or six months old I went to visit Ethel again but this time both Patty and Jane were there, after I had Tori, Jane had another baby daughter which meant that she had two children and I only had my one. When I went back to Ethel's house remembering that she did not even acknowledge my daughter the first time we visited her.

"What a cheek" I thought, when I went upstairs with my baby, Ethel sat there and had the nerve to ask me for my daughter telling me...

"I will adopt her, she will still know you as her mother but I will take care of her."

I knew that if I was stupid enough to let my little girl stay with this woman I would be signing my daughter up to be abused and I could not let that happen so I told her...

"No."

I thought that she got my message loud and clear but Ethel kept begging me for Tori, but I was adamant that I was not going to let that happen. Sulking to herself, the minute Jane walked into the room Ethel told her what she wanted from me, but just when I thought that I couldn't hear anymore cheek from this family, Jane's reply to me was...

"Yes give her to Ethel to bring up," I was balled over by what I was hearing from both of them I could not believe my ears, "Jane must have lost her mind to ask me such a question" I thought so I replied...

"You have two babies, you give her one of yours" and Jane said ...

"No, I want my two children" so my answer was...

"Just like you want your two, I want my one." And it ended like that or so I thought.

Two years later I became pregnant again with my second child, I was still living in the two bedroom flat when my daughter Stacey was born. Both Ethel and Raymond came to my home, unaware of their arrival, I opened the door and even though I had a newborn baby, I let them in (some would say that I was incredibly stupid or extremely forgiving), I did not let them come in any further than the kitchen we were all sitting around the kitchen table when Ethel was saying to Winston who was also there how she had been asking me for Tori and I refused her my baby.

I could not believe the audacity of the woman to even ask the man who has treated me so badly and to make things worse has not been there for my older daughter let alone my newborn for my daughter, at that point, I felt the strong urge to slap her and throw them out of my house but somehow I resisted, I thought that even if Winston had said yes Ethel and Raymond would not get their hands on my baby.

Her reason for still wanting Tori was...

"Now that Vanessa has another baby, I can take Tori and she can concentrate on Stacey." But I still was adamant that Ethel would not be getting Tori so my answer was still...

"No."

For the first time since we met, I felt that Winston was finally on my side, he said to Ethel...

"You give away things like chairs, tables e.t.c but you do not give away children so no."

"Thank God" I thought, that would save them all from an embarrassment and from that day, Ethel never asked for Tori even though I knew she had not let it go. Two years since I was living in my flat, my daily routine would consist of taking my children to Nursery and play group which they enjoyed but with no job, I was struggling financially, I needed help with the basic items for my children and household goods so I decided to ask Winston for his help and his answer was...

"No," with that in mind, I knew that I had to start saving which I did. One of the most important things that I needed in my house was a telephone so I saved up enough money to buy one for myself, when Winston came over he wanted to use my brand new phone, I had to remind him of his answer to me when I asked for his help, he then told me he would pay for his half of the phone bill, when I heard that, I allowed him to use my phone. Even though Winston promised that he would pay for his half of the phone bill, he never, so leaving me to take care of the unpaid bill.

By this time everything about this man got on my nerves, I reached the point where I got sick of him but that made no difference because Tori, Stacey and myself never saw this man, he was never there for any of his children, he would go away on weekends and holidays and we would not see him at all but

I could not allow that to bother me, I just had to continue with my life and raising both my daughters.

Stacey was just three to four months old when I was having problems with her going to sleep. One night Winston came around when Stacey was still awake and crying, not knowing the first thing about my baby or what was wrong with her, he slapped, I saw red and threw him out of my house but because he refused to leave, he slept in the store cupboard when he decided to apologise, I would not hear of it I just couldn't care less what he had to say.

Over the years, with everything that was going on, I became depressed because I had no one to talk to. As if I did not have a lot to deal with already, due to no fault of their own, Tori and Stacey developed a cold so I called the doctor and instead of him coming out to examine my girls, he prescribed their medicine over the phone, I shouldn't have given it to them knowing that he could not be bothered to examine my daughters but I was desperate and wanted to clear their colds. Tori recovered from her cold but my little Stacey became worse, it got so bad that she ended up in hospital because of it; I could not understand what was going on...

"Just a common cold," I thought "I did not realise that a simple medicine would affect my baby so badly, from a healthy 17lb baby to practically nothing she was looking so gaunt." I was scared stiff at the thought of losing my little girl. I thank God that her Nursery was weighing her and kept a record of it and also the health visitor had seen Stacey a week before the incident happened, she saw everything was ok, Stacey was in perfect health. But because the doctors at the hospital thought that I was mistreating my baby, they phoned her Nursery who then gave the hospital my daughter's records of how she was doing.

As weeks went by watching my daughter in the isolation ward, Stacey started to show signs of improvement; all this time I was telling the doctors that it was the medicine which had caused her to be so ill but they did not believe me so eventually when they had released Stacey from the hospital she had to go to the 'out patient 'department and that was when I found out Stacey had an infection which the medicine she had sparked it off because she was not given the right one by our GP.

Trying to put this nightmare behind me and move on with my life along with my daughters, one day Millie came to see me and told me that Winston the unforgivable father of both my daughters was saying really nasty things about me behind my back, both Leroy and Millie said that Winston was saying things like…

"When Vanessa was living with Rosa after Tori was born, I would leave Vanessa to go to work for 08:00 in the morning, the curtains undrawn and the bed unmade."

When I heard what Winston was saying about me I was really surprised and hurt just to think that this man was telling lies behind my back made me sick to my stomach, but what he failed to mention to his brother and sister in law was that when he did leave in the mornings, he would not return until 10:00pm or sometimes even later. Sitting there thinking about how out of order this man had been to me, I then went on to ask…

"If I was so bad why didn't Winston leave me and Leroy's reply was…

"I asked Winston the same thing."

During the conversation between Leroy, Millie and myself, I sat there thinking "This man who I thought loved me, how can he be so cruel?" I knew that I wanted to inflict revenge on him but for the sake of my children I had to rise above it.

I then asked Millie if she minded me confronting her brother in law about it and she said "No," so later on in the evening when Winston came around, I decided to confront him about everything that he had been saying to his family concerning me, watching the expression on his pathetic face, I knew that he was lying to me Winston also said to me that I was just as bad for mentioning it and not keeping quiet so I had to tell him that I was given permission by Millie to say something about it. While we were having a dispute about the whole thing all that was going through my mind is that I knew the minute we finished talking, Winston was going back to Melinda swearing and behaving badly, asking her why she opened her mouth and say anything to Millie. I believed that the very thought of Millie and Leroy having any loyalty to me was eating away at this man especially as Leroy was his brother. Of course my suspicions were right because Millie then phoned me to say that Winston had phoned Melinda swearing and having a go at her for opening her mouth but even though I knew what he was up to, Winston was still denying it.

Another two years later, I became pregnant for a third time at the age of twenty eight, giving birth to my third daughter at home and that was when everything came to ahead, not taking any more of what Winston was dishing out, to me it was the last straw, I threw his clothes outside on the door step I could not believe that the man I thought I knew was treating me this way, he was a deadbeat father never there for any of my kids, having an affair, I just could not stand to be around him any monger all I wanted to do was concentrate on my daughters.

When Dominique was nearly a year old, I got a bigger flat; it was a three bedroom in the same Borough but away from everyone. When Winston was not around I started packing my belongings for my new place, I had almost finished when he showed up, my new address was on the box and not remembering that it was there, he came in and saw that everything was taken down off the walls. Winston asked me where I was moving to but I did not tell him where I was going because I knew that if I had told him I would not be getting any peace from this man and that was not a thought that I relished very much that is all I wanted as far as I was concerned, we were finished but Winston was adamant in knowing where my children and I were moving to so he decided to snoop around to find our new address and without me knowing what he had done, Winston had found out where we were moving to.

My daughters and I had moved into our new property, I was so happy because I thought that we had finally got the peace that we always wanted, to move on with our lives until...

One day I heard the intercom, I went to answer it and I could not believe who was at the other end of the line, it was Winston so I asked him what he was doing at my flat and he answered...

"I would not bother you after today, I just want to buy you a cooker," even though it was a second hand cooker, the fact that he honoured his word and did it, it was something to me considering the fact that he could not be trusted.

Knowing Winston as well as I did, I knew that this was a ploy to get back into my life; I made my feelings perfectly clear, I did not want him back in my life because he was a pathological liar, a thief, a cheater and a gambler, couldn't hold down a job long enough and couldn't be bothered to pay child support for any of his kids, a man like that I could not allow around my daughters even though he needed to be because he had to fulfil his fatherly duties to them, spending time with the regardless of the fact that our relationship was over, Winston still had to be a father to his children a concept which he found extremely hard to grasp.

As my daughters were getting older, I found out that Winston had another daughter by someone else. My daughters were growing up so fast soon they were Nursery school, I wanted to teach them how to read so I asked Winston if he could buy them some reading books just to be told...

"No I would only get a theory book on driving for my other daughter." Not bothering to argue with him, I then decided to join a book club so that I could get the books that I needed for my girls to read Winston came back to ask me if I could buy some books for his other daughter but I wasn't going to let that happen, I had nothing against his other child simply because what her father had done wasn't her fault, I just couldn't bring myself to help him out when he constantly forgot about my three girls. They only had me because they never saw him, never got nearly as much as his other child and so because of that I felt that I needed to over compensate for their loss of a parent.

Chapter 7

I felt that I had jumped from the frying pan into the fire Winston was suffering from angina where he had to have two major operations which he was afraid of meanwhile despite all the feelings that I had felt for Ethel and Raymond, my children and I would travel to their house to do their cleaning, ironing, cooking e.t.c I would even cook dinner at my place and wrap it up for them knowing that they did not cook for themselves, this became a regular pattern for myself and three children while the other siblings did absolutely nothing to help their own parents.

I used to buy presents for my children, their father sometimes would buy them but not always and when he did, it was appreciated but being there for his kids was a hard task for him. Tori and Stacey was at the age where they were attending Primary School and Dominique was attending Nursery, it was perfect for me because I was able to go back to work and earn a proper living, because my hours were not based around my daughters properly, I asked Winston if he could watch the children while I was at work and he said to me...

"I will only watch them if you pay me." I could not believe that this man was standing there telling me that he would only keep an eye on his daughters if I paid him knowing that he was already working for himself so I decided to call it quits and stay home to look after my daughters myself adding to that, Winston also asked me to get the job for him instead but I was not having any if it.

My daughters were so young and full of energy they had three boxes filled with toys one for each of them which both myself and their father bought them on day Ethel and her husband came around to our place, hating the fact that my daughters had anything, Ethel said that Tori, Stacey and Dominique had too many toys so she decided to get a bin bag and empty the girls boxes leaving only one and a half boxes between them while Stacey and Dominique were in their rooms with her, Ethel's plans were to give my daughters toys to her other grandchildren despite the fact that they all had two parents who could provide for them and were perfectly capable of buying them toys for them selves which she did. Now Stacey and Dominique was scared of Ethel to say anything while Ethel was there because she treated my daughters the same way she treated me when I was younger so they waited until both Raymond and Ethel left.

When Stacey and Dominique told me what had happened, I was shocked and hurt just to know that Ethel has never bought anything for my children and then here she was coming into my house and stealing from my kids to give to the other grandchildren who also hated my daughters.

One day I had an accident which meant that I had to be admitted into hospital to have an operation, while I was there Jane, John and his wife lobbied for Tori, Stacey and Dominique to stay with Ethel and her husband until I got better and while they were staying there, I found out that Ethel had treated them so badly at their tender ages of seven, five and three, she would get them to wake up 06:00 in the morning to do the house work which would last virtually all day.

On one occasion she ordered Stacey to vacuum her stair case (the stairs in her house was very steep) being very little and at the age of five years old, Stacey could barely manage to do it so when she gave up Ethel called her into the living room and said really nasty things to her, she said…

"You are worthless do not bother inviting me to your house when you get older because you will keep it dirty."

Knowing how their mother behaved, Jane, John and his wife never went back to the house to check up on my girls, they were suffering behind closed doors at the hands of this vicious woman. Another time when Tori was having her bath Ethel accused her of lying about the towel, she beat Tori raw with the wet flannel. What happened was, I had a towel (a pink and white one) and when Tori, Stacey and Dominique went to stay with Ethel and Raymond they bought the white towel with them, Ethel was adamant that the towel was hers and when Tori tried to explain that it wasn't, that's when she beat her. Ethel would beat my daughters nearly everyday for one reason or the other it got to the point where they would come up in wheals and bruises, any and everything she would find to beat them with, it would range from huge belts to using her left fist because that was the hand where she wore her wedding rings and knowing that it would make maximum impact to hurt my girls.

Unaware of what was going on I still knew that my daughters were in danger so when Winston came to visit me, I told him to go and get my babies, when he was approaching the house, Tori, Stacey and Dominique was washing Raymond's car and when they saw him, they were thrilled at the thought that their father was coming to take them home.

When Winston came closer to the house, Tori, Stacey and Dominique started telling him about what Ethel had been doing to them and how Raymond would be in the next room with the television turned up so that he would not hear Ethel beating the hell out of them, when Winston heard everything that was going on he was so angry he could not believe this woman who calls herself a grandmother could treat his daughters so badly and that is why he hated her so much. Winston then told Tori, Stacey and Dominique to go upstairs and put some dry clothes on and also to pack because he was leaving with his children, but because Tori, Stacey and Dominique was so anxious to leave they wanted to go in their wet clothes but Winston had told them...

"No go and get some dry clothes on" so they went.

Chapter 8

Ethel has always said that Stacey looked like me and sometimes Dominique which is why I felt that it was the reason Ethel treated them the way that she did. Ethel never cared how she behaved towards them she would buy multi-packs of crisps for her grandchildren, leave them in her car boot when she forgot to hand them out and when the crisps expired then she would give them to Tori, Stacey and Dominique to eat but I always told them not to eat the crisps because they will become sick.

Another family member who started to show signs of turning into her mother is Patty, Patty would sit down and talk about myself and three children especially Dominique to everyone outside and within the family, which is why they had a pre-conceived notion of us putting them off the idea of getting to know us for them selves. Patty would cause problems for us and tell her brothers that we were the ones who did it, making us look like we are the bad guys in all of this, "It was like Ethel all over again," I thought to myself.

As far as I was concerned, Patty was not off the hook either, I remember I needed a place of my own and I asked her to look after my cutleries and glasses until I found a place, when the time came for me to get my property back from her, I found out that her and her family was using them and broke my glasses which she didn't even repay me for. Realising that there was nothing that I could do about it no matter how hard I tried, there was no way that I could get my things back nor would she repay me for the broken items so I decided to let it go.

Patty is the kind of person that would undermine my authority when it came to my own children, when ever they had a problem with someone that they knew, and it came out in the open, Patty would go straight to her brothers to sort it out instead of coming to me, I would always be the very last person to find out what had happened to my children. I would be so angry because I knew that if it was her child that was involved in any dispute, she would want to be the first to know about it and her daughter is much older than my first daughter.

The whole situation between the family and us became so bad it became transparent, everyone could see that we were treated differently from the others, the bad treatment would start from Ethel and Raymond, go straight

down to the children and then finally down to the grandchildren, they would all pick up the bad habit which meant that my children and I were the only ones left out of the family circle.

One day some one outside of the family said to me...

"I notice that Ethel treats your kids differently from the other grandchildren," she also said that...

"I told Kingston's wife because I know that she will chat" (Kingston's wife was known as a chatterbox). Her aim was to let Kingston or anyone else in the family know how Ethel treated my daughters whenever there were family gatherings for events like Boxing Day, my children and I would dread going because we knew that we were going to be isolated from the others and be in the kitchen washing up after the rest of them (including the in-laws) with no help, but knowing that they would make us feel incredibly guilty for not turning up, we would then decide to go just to keep the peace. On one particular Boxing Day, we were invited to a 'family' gathering knowing how things were between us, my children and I drank a few bottles of wine (to numb the pain) before showing up, it just so happened that we ended up a little drunk because of it that was the only way we could get through the day around them.

All we wanted to do was be alone and enjoy Christmas by ourselves and not with people who could only manage to love and remember us for one day out of the year. My daughters and I were perfectly fine in our old flat, we hardly saw the family, life was great apart from your usual bullying that my children had to suffer with, everything else was ok.

I am not sure how it happened exactly but when Tori, Stacey and Dominique was attending school, the men in the family along with Patty got involved with our housing by writing various letters to the housing on my behalf on Ethel's orders, her reason for them doing this was for my children and I to be closer to the family and behind our backs they had us transferred to East London by the time I found out there was nothing that I could do so

I was left with the only option to move with my children which was a huge mistake that was ever made in our lives.

They got us moved from a council flat into a private rented accommodation where we were constantly having problems with the various landlords.

Chapter 9

We moved into our new area when Dominique had just turned eight years old, we were now living not too far from some of them. We believed that the only reason for them wanting us closer is so they could spy on us and to use us as 'in house' slaves because they felt that we had nothing to do in our lives personally they looked down on us and because Tori, Stacey and Dominique is mixed race, born out of wed lock and have no father who is around, they feel that my daughters are beneath them all and so my kids start to think the same way.

Ethel was so happy that we moved to East London because it meant that we were at her beckon call, at least four days out of the seven, we would be at Ethel's and Raymond's house cleaning, cooking, washing their dirty dishes, ironing and other household chores that you can imagine, we would be there

from around 09:00 / 10:00 in the morning and we would not leave until 7:00 or 8:00 in the evening feeling tired and exhausted, any other day that we wanted for ourselves was out of the question because Ethel would get Raymond to call us just so we could go down there to clean her house some more even though my daughters and I never understood how two people can make so much mess in so little time that they needed us virtually everyday of the week.

Going around to different houses to help out was getting out of hand because John and his wife who are both able to look after what goes on in their own home had the nerve to ask me to stay at their home and wait for the television company to arrive (not even asking me whether I am busy that day or not)

"Like I don't have better things to do with my time" I thought "They didn't even have the courtesy to ask me if I was busy." They just assumed that I wasn't doing anything with my time, so like an idiot, I went, knowing that John's wife had gone out for the day but assured me that she would be back at 1:00 in the afternoon, Tori offered to come along with me while Stacey and Dominique was at school. Back at John and his wife's house, Tori and I were waiting for the television company to arrive but no one turned up while we were there, out of the kindness of my heart I washed their dirty dishes and cleaned their kitchen. Eventually John's wife turned up late in the evening having the cheek to ask me...

"What's for dinner," I was fuming with her because I wanted to go home and she didn't have the manners to apologise for be so late but anyway I did not say anything to her because as far as I was concerned, this woman was not worth my time or energy so Tori and I had to walk back home in the rain in the dark (pitch black) without an offer of a lift home from her or even a thank you.

My daughters and I started to feel like everyone's employee, we could not get the chance to get on with our own lives but we knew one of the reasons why they were acting like that towards us. One day Tori, Stacey, Dominique and I were told by someone outside the family that what she heard from a member of the family is this...

"All Vanessa's kids are good for is to hold people's bags." (Implying that they would not be good enough only to be slaves for other people).

I was hurt by what I heard but as always there was nothing that I could say or do because my daughters and I could not trust any one even though I mentioned it to Kingston and Melvin their typical comments were...

"We do not believe that anyone would say that."

Trying to protect my kids from the heartache that I went through as a child growing up it became impossible after hearing a lot of negative comments from the family and school kids, Tori, Stacey and Dominique lost their self-esteem which meant that they became less confident in themselves believing that they were not worth very much and the way our lives was starting to turn out, they themselves were starting to believe it and as a result, they were too scared to take a risk in life.

With no family members to count on and no father to speak of I didn't bother telling Winston where we had moved to due to his disgusting behaviour while my daughters and I were living in our flat. Winston would come to the flat drunk, banging on the door and screaming for me to let him in after I put the girls to bed, I did not appreciate it especially as it was difficult for

Stacey because she did not seem to like going to sleep, he was making a lot of noise

and waking them up in the middle of the night it happened again on one particular weekend where we had someone staying with us, she became afraid of him. I was not about to let Winston in my home because I was scared for my daughters I did not know what this man was capable of in his drunken state so I did not let him in that night, many more disturbing events followed after this one concerning Winston, his promises to take Tori to see her older sister but never living up to his promise, that is why I did not inform him of my whereabouts to a new part of London.

My daughters had not seen their father in over four years, maybe more and even though they were lacking in that father figure, I tried to be everything that they needed sometimes it wasn't enough. One day Winston rang Ethel to ask for our new address so that he could send Tori some birthday presents and for the first and only time that woman had done something right, she told him…

"No." She suggested that he send Tori's presents to her house and she would forward them to my address but nothing came so I knew that he had no intention of sending Tori anything it was a ploy to get my new address.

Years went by and things became quiet where Winston was concerned then one Tuesday evening Tori, Stacey, Dominique and I was sitting down in the living room watching television when out of the blue, Ethel rang and told me something that I knew I would find extremely difficult to deliver to my children she told me…

"I have some bad news," I was afraid to hear what was coming next until I heard those words that I would never forget "Winston died." I was shocked, I could not believe what I was hearing but I knew that the worst was to come , telling my girls that their father had died so when I got off the phone to Ethel, I gathered my children and gently broke the news to them, Tori instantly broke down and went to pieces crying uncontrollably, Stacey and Dominique did not say anything so I did not know what was going through their minds at the time as far as I remember they really did not cry the first time I told them, it must have been shock.

Even though I now realised that the man I first loved and thought loved me was no longer walking or talking, my main priority was and always my children (even more so now) and being there for them, helping them overcome their grief that they were feeling.

As the days went by Tori showed no sign of getting better a non family member offered to keep Tori until she got over her grief, I agreed because I did not know what to do and I figured that a non relative could help her instead maybe she would open up, while the black cloud was looming over our household not one of my so called brothers and sisters picked up the phone to find out how their sister and nieces were doing none of my daughters cousins sent any sympathy their way, all the comments my daughters got from the family is…

"You didn't even know him so why are you crying." And that comment came from one of their cousins who was supposed to be supportive.

"Talk about kicking them when they are down" I thought even if my kids didn't know their father as well as they know theirs, it didn't give them the right to talk about my children that way. Just when the lack of compassion couldn't

get any worse, my daughters were compared to some other kids who had a father; I could not believe the callousness from the very same people who carries the same name as my daughters and call them selves family as far as we were concerned, these people were not family after the sudden death of Winston, I realised the new level of how cold and unfeeling these people were, truly I did not know any of them. The day of the funeral had arrived a day that we were all dreading but we had to pluck up the courage and go, the service went pretty quickly and then everyone went outside for family photos, that was when Tori, Stacey, Dominique and I saw for the very first time, my daughters sister Leanne who did not know about her three younger sisters or what they looked like.

After the funeral I was left to comfort my girls on my own leaving me with very little time to grieve on my own. My daughters did not know a lot of their relatives on their father's side, their grandparents died before they were born, they were kept a secret from their sister and the rest of the relatives were unable to see my daughters because Ethel's family tried their very best to stop them from seeing my daughters which I would not put up with when I did know about it.

One day Maggie came to East London and asked if she could spend the day with her nieces which they all enjoyed very much because that meant Tori, Stacey and Dominique did not have to see Ethel's side of the family for at least one day when Tori, Stacey and Dominique returned, the family was so angry and jealous but I didn't care what they thought or felt, my daughters needed a bit of fun in their lives after everything that they had been through and if Ethel's family were not going to be there for them, I did not want to know.

"Tori, Stacey and Dominique have other uncles, aunts and cousins besides these ones and if they want to take them out to enjoy themselves, it has nothing to do with Ethel's side of the family" I thought.

As the years went by and time had healed, my daughters and I tried to pick up the pieces and move on with our lives, over many years of suffering at the hands of Ethel's family, my daughters started to feel alienated, inferior, foreign and treated in a very cold and calculating manner from their uncles and aunts, racially abused and disrespected from their cousins because they are the only ones in the family who are mixed race, my daughters wrote a letter to the uncles, aunts and to Ethel explaining how they were making them feel, it was a big mistake on some levels because the guys ripped into my children saying the most nastiest things to them.

Paul said, "I am not their father." As we could clearly see, but surely it wouldn't have made a difference if he was there for them as that male figure. The rest of them started talking about all the things that they had bought us even though they all knew that wasn't what my daughters were talking about, they were talking about the emotional side of the relationship as far as my daughters were concerned, they needed that balance in their lives and trying to find it somewhere, they obviously went looking in the wrong place.

Kingston sat there until the end and when everything was said and done, he told us that he took another girl who was in a similar situation as my girls out for a day to make her feel loved despite the fact that she was one of the nasty ones who hated my daughters especially Stacey for some unknown reason

which she admitted to. Without saying much Kingston had just proven our point but knowing that we were not going to get anywhere with them and this pointless meeting, John who had absolutely nothing to do with the letter situation decided to involve himself so it was the four of us versus them all needless to say, we left it at that, leaving them to it that was when Patrick admitted to me that the family was indeed dysfunctional and at that point I did not want to hear what he had to say I thought that he had the perfect opportunity to say it in the meeting but he was too chicken to stand up and speak his mind because he was the kind of guy who would rather stick with the crowd (even though he knows the truth), than admit the truth, I just couldn't bare to look at him any longer let alone her the rest of garbage that was coming out of hi mouth, I was extremely angry with the fact that he let his brothers rip into my children and I knowing that he felt the same way and did nothing to help.

Not wanting to be disturbed by them, my daughters and I continued to live our lives the way we wanted, we did not want anything to do with them after they all made themselves perfectly clear on how they felt, my daughters are incredibly independent and that is what others could not stand, Tori, Stacey and Dominique find it hard to have people think for them let alone talk for them, they would not put up with it, they cannot stand it when they are told what to do when they know that they are capable of doing something on their own, but the other grandchildren, (as proven) are not as independent as my ones simply because of the two very different lives that they have all lived.

Not only were they lacking in independence but they were also very immature from the eldest one right to the youngest one. On one occasion John's older son Caleb started a fight with Tori, blowing it out of proportion and causing her to have an asthma attack, when the whole fight finally ended his father started calling my children liars but he failed to realise that it was his kids and Melvin's older daughter who were doing all the lying. There was nothing that he could do when everyone told the story exactly how Tori, Stacey and Dominique told it but when it came for him to apologise,

John never did, no apology for calling my daughters a liar, neither did his boy apologise for troubling Tori and causing her asthma.

Everything was going wrong in our lives; the family was not making it any easier for us. On one occasion I found out something that had crushed me, I found out that my beautiful daughters had been sexually abused when they were younger I almost died to find out what had been going on behind my back again, with no support from my 'family' but intense grief, the only words of comfort that Patty had to say to me was...

"If you had sent them to stay with their grandparents, this would never have happened."

"How dare her "I thought "What the hell was this woman on about, my children were hurt and all she could think about was me not sending them to their grandparents."

"Why is my family the only ones getting hurt and others are ok, we have done nothing wrong so why us" I thought. This was the last straw, everything that could have happened to my daughters and I happened "How were we going to bounce back from this another mind blowing situation to deal without support from Ethel's family, who I no longer needed in my life but could not

get away from. Not willing to help and support me in my hour of need but the minute a problem arose concerning my daughter's and I, Patty would be on the phone to Jane spreading my business, if that wasn't bad enough Jane would go and tell someone else who had nothing to do with the family our personal problems, it went around to everyone who was willing to listen (and everyone was willing to listen), I would eventually hear about it. I did not know who to trust when I looked around all I could see was a community of people who had betrayed me in one way or the other.

In 2003 my daughters were old enough, Tori was twenty, Stacey was eighteen and Dominique was sixteen years old, I had a major operation because of my anaemia, it was so bad that the doctor had to refer me as an urgent patient because if I did not get this problem sorted out, I could have suffered with heart failure and died which was not an option for me because I could not leave my kids with no parents even though they were old enough. Eventually I was admitted into hospital where I spent 5 days re-cooperating, Tori, Stacey and Dominique were so good, everyday without fail, they would be at the hospital until the very day when I was discharged (even though they forgot my clothes, I had to go home in my pyjamas), I went home to finish recovering from the major operation that I had just to be re admitted when I was feeling some stabbing pains under my ribs, I was given blood thinning injection and under very careful supervision.

The next day I was allowed to go back home but before I went, I was under strict instructions not to do any heavy lifting and basically taking it easy by remaining on bed rest I agreed to the conditions and went on my way with my kids waiting for me, I reached my front door for the second time and I was so happy to finally be home again with my babies who took very good care of me. Everyone knew about my operation and even though most of them came to visit me in the hospital, it didn't stop Ethel ringing me months later asking for me to go to her home and clean, Tori, Stacey and Dominique was very angry at what she was asking of me because they knew that when "Patty was having her operation she went away to Jane's to re-cooperate without anyone bothering her so why did Ethel have to bother our mum" they thought," can't she leave her alone to recover in peace " there was nothing that my daughters could do to prevent them from bothering me so I had no choice but to go to Ethel's and Raymond's house to do the housework, feeling sorry for me, my daughters decided to go with me, we were doing work that men should have been doing and the fact that Ethel has eleven male grandchildren, she could have easily asked one of them to help her out but instead she felt that Stacey, Dominique, Tori and I needed the extra muscles even though I was not in a fit state to do any heavy lifting.

Dominique, Tori, Stacey and I felt that Ethel was taking advantage of our good and kind nature, we are the kind of people that loves to help others even if it means going out of our way to do so, Ethel knew it so she took full advantage, we did not complain (which we really should have) we just carried on with it. One day we were at their house doing the cleaning, another one of John's boys was also at the house, being a lazy person that Jamie is, he sat around and never lifted a finger to help us with the housework, I mean after all he is

Ethel's grandson, he left the entire work up to Dominique and myself telling Dominique that it is a woman's job and even though he felt that way,

Raymond paid him £40 for doing nothing and we didn't even get as much as a thank you for your time and help.

Dominique, Tori, Stacey and I cried on a number of occasions because of our family members, recapping over what they all done to us I remembered when I was younger before I left home and had my daughters. I owned a skirt and waistcoat which I wore as a two piece, I remember wanting the jacket to go with it so that it would complete the entire suit, one day Jane came home with the jacket to my two piece suit she told me that she did not like that jacket and that she was planning on taking it back to the shop, I told Jane that I wanted the jacket because it matched my waistcoat and skirt so with that in mind, I offered to buy it from her I said to her...

"Instead of taking it back let me buy it off you." I then asked her how much the jacket cost and she told me "£20"

After hearing my offer, Jane still decided to take the jacket back to the shop and get her money refunded knowing that I wanted it and was willing to buy it from her, "How spiteful" I thought to myself so I then decided to ask her to tell me where she purchased the jacket so that I could go and buy it myself. I finally had my jacket that I always wanted but not for long, I do not know what was going through Jane's mind at the time but she saw my jacket, borrowed it and never gave it back, I remember that I kept asking her for it back but she was always giving me feeble excuses so I asked her for my £20 but she had no intention of reimbursing me with neither my jacket or my £20.

"Maybe it's the thought of me having something new that bothered her so much" I told myself, I needed to tell myself anything that I thought would comfort me because I just couldn't comprehend the cruelty of Jane's actions. Five years after the incident happened, I had forgotten all about it, by that time Jane was married, I never knew why, but she was bragging and laughing to her husband about what she had done to me five years ago without a remorseful bone in her body. Thinking that she was going to get praised for it, her husband said to her...

"You are wicked for what you done."

Chapter 10

TORI'S STORY

When my sisters and I were younger, living in South London we were very happy, nothing seemed to bother us even though we were bullied. As we got older Stacey, Dominique and I had become very resourceful, there was never a time when we didn't know how to entertain ourselves. I t was not until we moved up in East London when the problems started, like our mother, we found ourselves at the mercy of others especially the family; it drove us to lose every bit of our confidence and self-esteem.

You wouldn't believe that a family as large as ours could be so cruel, people outside has always seen the fascination of the family but to us it has been a different story, you would have a lot of women running to marry the boys of the family but only us four was running to get out, we would try anything even if it meant changing our surnames, the cousins are so competitive no matter

what my sisters and I did they would take it that we were competing against them which as far as my sisters and I were concerned, we were not bothered with all that rubbish, it got to the point where it had a major affect on us as individuals and collectively and the way people started to see us, as far as other people were concerned, my sisters and I lost all our individual identities.

For the next five years my mum, sisters and I was living in a private rented accommodation until it was time for us to leave, we moved into another property where the tenancy agreement was for two years due to the fact that the Landlord's sister was working abroad for the duration of time. During all the family problems my mum was also having issues with our schooling because of racism that was going on in our secondary schools, the housing departments who was messing her around, she just did not have the strength to deal with everything at once but something that I should have told her and that was she did just fine in her situation, I cannot imagine it being very easy as a single parent trying to be both mother and father as well as coping with everyday life including what the family was throwing at her.

As two years was approaching, my mum got a phone call from the Landlord's sister saying that she wanted her property back because she was pregnant and needed her place back which meant that we were on the hunt for another house again (a problem that we didn't have to deal with had the family left us alone in South London). The day of the move, it was Stacey's 17th birthday a day filled with unwanted memories; we were standing outside our property not knowing where to go, that was when someone from the Education Department came to the house and started asking my mum questions about our housing situation, she tried to tell the lady that we had to move again but unsure of where it was we were going (the Housing Dept knew that the tenancy agreement was for two years but they did nothing to help us find another accommodation to live until the very last day), so the lady then told my mum that when we do eventually know where it is that we are going, Dominique should apply for a school near that location, so a few weeks before she had to finish school in definitely, Dominique was kicked out due to no fault of her own.

We eventually ended up in a small smelly dark dinghy one room (which we later found out was a store cupboard) Bed & Breakfast, because it was in a devastating state, all we could do was cry after a few minutes of weeping we tried to pull ourselves together and try to make the best of a bad situation while thinking of ways to get out of it. "How could this happen to us," we all thought "We were living happily in a huge council flat in another part of London, the family decided to interfere and bring us all the way up to this part of London just to end up in a dinghy Bed & Breakfast." The thought of us living in this place was scary because it was the first time that we ever encountered something as horrible as this.

Trying to do the best that we could under the circumstances, it was proving very difficult because the room in itself was extremely dark, there was only one small window which was barred up, we could not use the kitchen or the bathroom because they were so filthy, all we had was a small basin to wash ourselves in. It was like living in a cave or underground, whenever we left the building our eyes would pull due to the bright sunlight, we hardly got any sleep due to the horrendous noise that other people were making right outside our room. The whole thing was so uncomfortable for us but we tried to manage somehow.

One night as we were going to bed, my mum and Stacey were horrified to see what they saw, there on the bed lay a fat limy maggot, they tried to take a picture of it so that we could complain but because the room was so dark and they did not have a camera with a flash light, the films never developed. Knowing that we could not continue living like this anymore, we complained to the ombudsman and after two long gruelling months in the Bed & Breakfast, we left to live in another one which was infested with rats and mice.

After spending eight months in the second Bed & Breakfast, my family and I had finally moved into another private rented accommodation, it wasn't ideal because the house was falling apart. Looking around our new home, we thanked God that it was our home nonetheless.

"There is no way that we can settle down because we have to move again," that was the thought looming at the back of our minds. As time went by our front door would get stuck so we had to leave it ajar, we couldn't open and shut the door because it would not move so our only mode of getting in and out the house was through the window.

Afraid that one day someone might think that we were breaking in, it was a risk that we had no choice but to take, there was no point in complaining to the Landlord because he wouldn't have done anything to sort the problem out like he has failed to do with many things that went wrong in the house. Elsewhere, problems for us between our so called family members and friends never improved, it got to the point where Stacey, Dominique and I grew incredibly close, no one could penetrate it and because of that, people started to look and treat us as though we were freaks, they became scared and intimidated by our closeness because they did not understand.

There were occasions where my sisters and I were asked questions and we'd come out with the identical answers at the same time, cousins, in-laws, friends whoever it was, always thought that how we would answer people was bizarre but it wasn't because we were weird, it's just that no one wanted to get to know us, they didn't like us at all.

My mum, sisters and I thought their problem was because Dominique, Stacey and I is very intelligent and mature especially from a very young age due to not having a father it forced us to grow up very quickly, the petty things that other kids would make a fuss about, we were not bothered with, no one could deny the fact that we were mature for our ages it was something that Stacey, Dominique and I was told constantly because it was so obvious.

Chapter 11

STACEY'S STORY

Problems were rapidly mounting for my daughters and I, more than we liked, it was to the point where it had spiralled out of control, things got unbelievably worse and it did not help with the fact that we had a group of unsupportive family members who interfered and ruined the rest of our lives.

The day we moved to East London, my children and I were constantly moving around from home to home for various reasons never able to settle down. I was now at the age where I wanted to meet someone else and get married because I was feeling lonely, I love my children but I wanted them to go off and be teenagers not constantly worrying about me, they had already lost out on their childhood, I did not want them to lose out on their teenage years as well, but sadly enough they lost out on their teenage years.

Because we were moving around so much, after eight years of moving to three different private rented accommodations and two Bed & Breakfast's we eventually got a place where we thought that we would call our own, believing that it was a start to something new and different and a settled life we started planning to make up for lost time by trying new things. Tori, Stacey and Dominique started taking up extra curricular activities like Karate which they were all enjoying very much, at the same time Stacey and

Dominique was also attending and adult college to finish studying French again and Dancing all of which they enjoyed until it had to come to an end when they could no longer afford to keep going, but when it came to the dance classes, Ethel and Raymond got in the way because on the same day that Dominique and Stacey was due to go to their dance class, we all got a phone call from Ethel saying that they needed help with their house so out of the kindness of our hearts, we dropped what we were doing to go and help them out.

After all these years of manipulation and control from the family, my children and I got fed up with it all and decided not to allow them to continue taking over our lives, we tried to take control or our own lives. But it was not all good because going to church on Sundays (where they were giving us grief) it was quite difficult to let go completely, my children and I felt as though we were constantly under a microscope, maybe to an extent we were. There would always be competition between the grandchildren and other kids towards my daughters, everything my girls had, they wanted no matter what it took for them to get it, it would range from priceless materials to the opposite sex, it was so pathetic with the aid of their parents both my girls lost out anyway.

Stacey's story

I remember a guy who Tori grew up with, she loved him very much and he felt the same way, it was like a match made in heaven between the both of them they were like the perfect couple, everyone knew how they felt about each other even they themselves knew although it was indirectly, being young and in love, they were also very shy and Tori couldn't admit how she felt to Andy, but the blissful relationship ended when Patty's daughter Nancy who is much

older than both Tori and Andy, started to get involved (because she too had feelings for Andy) and chasing Andy around, everywhere he was she would be there, the thing is, Andy never shared the same feelings towards Nancy as he did for Tori but nothing was going to stop her, as far as Nancy was concerned she knew what she wanted and was going to get it no matter who was in her way and regardless of how Andy felt.

Tori on the other hand being the quiet and reserved person (maybe a little too reserved) she tried to play it cool, my mum, Dominique and I was helping her to get the man that we all knew she wanted but despite all our efforts, Nancy

was too much to handle, it wasn't so bad because we all knew that Andy couldn't stand the sight of Nancy but that never seem to put her off, I guess she must have thought that she could change his mind which we all knew wasn't going to happen.

Andy is the kind of person that when he makes up his mind, he refuses to change so that was working in our favour, the whole thing started to feel like we were competing but feeling tired of the way the family behaved, my mum, Dominique and I couldn't stand by and watch Nancy win (so to speak) she did not know how to exhibit any pride in herself.

The pressure must have gotten too much for Andy where Nancy was concerned and with Tori holding back how she felt about him, he decided to leave which meant that both Tori and Nancy lost out he decided to go for someone else which broke Tori's heart even though she never admitted it to us, we knew that she was disappointed when he left.

As for me, I was touring around the UK with the choir when I met someone, he was the drummer who was playing for our choir, ideally, he wasn't what I wanted which is why I never really thought about it at first, a few weeks later one of the gigs we did, Jay, Tori, Dominique and I was sitting in the van talking and laughing, it must have been his personality and his ability to make me laugh (a quality in a man that I never realised I needed very much until then) which brew me to him.

Months after, we were still hanging around each other, everyone, namely the cousins could see that he was drawn to me and felt the need to interfere even married women was after him once again by getting his number to call or text him and when they saw that we were together, they would call him over just so he would stay away, I was determined that they were not going to win this time and once again Dominique, my mum and Tori was helping. Finding it difficult to spend time with Jay because people were always around asking questions and trying to mess things up. Feeling that if they couldn't have him, they would rather ruin the whole thing instead.

As months by and the more time we spent, feelings started to get a little more serious and despite everything that was going on, it felt right, it was strange because even though I felt way, it wasn't until four months later when I realised that I had feelings for Jay I guess it was because it happened so quickly and totally out of my character. There were times when I had questioned my feelings and if they were real but I always came back to the same answer "Yes they were real, I loved him and I wanted to marry him."

It did not last long because everyone was getting involved including married women, Patrick's daughter who was rude to him saying things like…

"Why are you always hanging around my cousins" Tori, Dominique and myself knew that he was uncomfortable at that point which is why he backed off but then after we spoke to him everything went back to normal.

The whole thing was getting ridiculous because you would have some who would put pressure on Jay and others throwing themselves at him and making sure that I was not going to get Jay, they ran him off. After Jay left, Patrick's daughter told Tori, Dominique and I, that Jay had got another girl pregnant, her aim was to get a reaction out of one of us to see which one of us had feelings for Jay which I thought was cruel, hiding my feelings so well, she

stupidly thought that it was Dominique, "she couldn't have been so far off the mark, "I thought to myself but I wasn't about to let her know that.

After all the commotion, Tori, Dominique and I, had made a deal with each other that enough was enough and that we were going to mess the others up for what they had done even though we did not mean physically, but emotionally and mentally just to teach them a lesson that what they had done was wrong and that Jay was the last straw but then events took a different turn which meant that we separated from them.

We were so happy that for the first time in our lives we didn't have anyone to bother us especially as it saved the skins of the cousins because what we had planned would have been disastrous, we were planning on causing irreparable damage but we were free from everyone or so we thought...

Chapter 12

After four years in our home, months passed when everything started to go wrong again, it started out that the job which Tori and Stacey was working in for two years, they were forced to quit but around the time that they were working, a few problems had risen between us, the Benefit Office and the company who we were renting our home from, it got to the point where misunderstandings happened due to simple errors that were made with Tori and Stacey's wages. Spending months trying to sort out the situation, my children and I lost the fight in keeping our home.

So we spent the Christmas Holidays taking everything off the walls and packing to leave once again. In early January where it was cold and frosty, my daughters and I were left completely and utterly homeless with no where to go and no one to help.

"How comes everyone else succeeds in life and all we get is problems" this was a question that we would often ask ourselves. Not understanding how our lives turned out like this again but this time even worse, we tried to keep our chins up and plod on for the sake of our sanity "Whatever happens, our so called family cannot know about our situation." This was a mutual understanding that Tori, Dominique, Stacey and I had because we knew that

they had already looked down on us and we didn't want to give them more cause to continue.

With very little option on where to go, we could only stay at our friends' house for the maximum of three days due to the fact that they were having a baby and not to overstay our welcome, we decided to leave after three days even though they were happy to help us out. Everyday, my daughters and I would walk the streets trying to find a place to live but it was proving very difficult with the horrible weather and the un kindness of people, no one was willing to open up their shelters to us. So we had no money, no where to go and not many people would help. There would be nights when Tori, Dominique, Stacey and I would be wandering the streets trying to find a place to sleep, one night we were standing in the freezing cold when a young man walked up to us offering to let us stay at his flat for two nights we were reluctant at first but with no other alternative, we decided to take him up on his offer.

Back at the flat, we were so tired and wanted to sleep, he was forcing us to eat even though we were telling him that we just wanted a rest but he wasn't taking no for an answer, he held a knife to me ordering me to eat, my daughters and I were so scared the next day we left and never returned to his place. Other nights it was so impossible to keep our heads above water when things were not going the way we wanted, some days Tori, Dominique, Stacey and I were ok and other days we'd have a nervous breakdown, we were so frightened to be wandering the streets at night. Another night, we were sitting on a bench when a lady came up to us and asked...

"Why are you sitting there? if you stay out here, you will die," my daughters and I were not too surprised at what the lady said because it was extremely frosty but because there was nothing that we could do, it did not make any sense in trying until a young man came up to us and asked us... "Why are you all sitting out here?" we told him that we had no where else to go so his reply to us was... "I have a sister and I could not see her out on the streets" with that, he gave us a cup of tea to warm us up and offered us his place to stay for the night, we kindly agreed. As we were walking towards the house Dominique, Tori, Stacey and I was so grateful for the temporary roof which was for one night, as we reached the house, we sat down I the living room we could hear his mother telling him off for allowing us to stay, she said to him "They can't stay here tell them to leave," after hearing what his mother said, there was no way that we could stay there for the night so we left.

Dominique, Stacey, Tori and I were terribly distressed by what was going on, one night we were sitting down in McDonalds and all of a sudden we burst out into crying, after the random crying fest was over, we started to wander the streets again deliriously when we saw Kingston driving up to us wanting to know why we were out so late, sitting in the car, we were so embarrassed he took us to his house where he phoned for a Bed & Breakfast, we stayed at the Bed & Breakfast for six days and nights pondering over the fact that sooner or later these people were going to be in our business again making us feel like failures because of the situation that we were in, a thought which did not please us very much but had to deal with then one night we got a phone call

from Kingston he was telling us that he was going to drive us to Ethel and Raymond's house because apparently they had agreed to us staying there until we got a place of our own, this was a decision that we were sceptical about because we were not in a position to on where to stay, we had no choice, we had to live with the idea that nearly cost us our sanity.

Arriving at Ethel and Raymond's home, it was awkward for two reasons, one because they had not seen us in a year and two, their hatred for us became intensified. Because it was their home, Tori, Dominique, Stacey and I had to mind our P's and Q's, constantly walking around on eggshells until three days later trouble was brewing (Ethel going to bed arguing and waking up arguing), early in the morning, everything was getting on top of us emotionally when Ethel came into the bedroom that we were sleeping in and started complaining, that was when Stacey said to herself "I can't deal with this any more."

Perfectly innocent, Ethel started shouting at her and behaving badly so Stacey, knowing that she was not going to hear the last of the argument went and apologised to Ethel for what she had said, Ethel never accepted her

apology (Ethel must have phoned John behind our backs) but later on in the day John who we had not seen in over four years came to the house with such a bad attitude towards us because of the things that Patty was telling him behind our backs. So when he came to the house, Ethel, Raymond and John went into the kitchen to whisper about us she was saying that we were making her feel uncomfortable and that we had put her out by staying there, she also told him about the incident earlier on in the morning despite the fact that Stacey apologised to her, something that she conveniently forgot to mention to him, her aim was to cause trouble (and trouble she caused), her plan was successful because when John heard what was going on, his answer to his mother was...

"Why didn't you let them stay on the streets?" (totally disregarding everything that we had been through) he also said to her that he was going to talk to us about it, she kept telling him no but we believed that she was saying it for our benefit trying to make us think that she did not want to cause trouble when we all know her better than she thought she was telling him "No."

Ignoring her plea, John approached the bedroom where we were and started shouting and insulting me, the argument became increasingly intense so Tori tried to calm me down, John took one look at Tori and pushed her, he them turned to me and started pushing me also, after he finished with the both of us, he turned to Dominique and started pointing his finger in her face when she wasn't even in the argument (meanwhile Ethel standing back and loving the argument, just the thought of her son coming to her rescue), so with all that going on Tori, Dominique, Stacey and I started to pack our belongings and leave Ethel's house stunned at the fact that she had purposely orchestrated the whole thing so that it would blow completely out of proportion which had turned into a violent altercation.

As we were leaving Ethel's home, she was asking us where were we going, meaning to give the silent treatment, we left with out saying a word to her.

Back on the streets, a place that we were dreading but at least we had some peace and quiet, we were back to square one, Tori, Dominique, Stacey and I was wandering the streets for three days when Patty phoned us wanting to call a truce (yeah right!) Tori, Dominique, Stacey and I were sitting in the library when we got the phone call; we decided if we should listen to her and call a truce, conclusion was "Might as well."

So with that, Patty asked us where we were staying and because we had no where else to go, Patty drove us back to the house of hell.

That Monday night when we returned to Ethel's place another argument erupted that same night.

Chapter 13

The morning after the big argument between Ethel and myself, the atmosphere in the house was some what frosty; Ethel was not speaking to me at all at the same time being very cold and distant towards Stacey and Dominique, she would never treat Tori the way she treats Dominique, Stacey and I because Ethel has always preferred Tori to her sisters. We were very grateful for the temporary roof over our heads, but not at the expense of our happiness and sanity.

Everyday it got more and more impossible to live in that house, (it was almost like we had regressed), Ethel and Raymond did not feel like family to us or vice versa, but being the kind of people that my daughters and I are, we tried to overlook the problem and try to respect them in their own home. One of the things that my daughters and I agreed to do was buy our own food which we did, everything apart from what we couldn't help was separated. One day Ethel went out and not knowing what time she would be back or if she was going to be too tired to cook her dinner, Stacey kindly started cooking the chicken that she had left out for Ethel and her husband (which he was suppose to be cooking himself). Before Stacey started cooking the chicken, she asked Raymond how they liked it to be cooked and his reply was...

"Cook it the same way that you cook yours," so she did, when Ethel got back from her outing, she went straight into the kitchen to find the chicken in the oven, instead of a simple thank you, Ethel went totally ballistic and started ripping into Stacey for cooking the chicken, Stacey tried to explain that Raymond was the one who told her to cook it the same way she cooked hers but Ethel was not having any of it, when Raymond heard that Ethel was shouting at Stacey, he took that opportunity to escape into the living room so that he would not have to deal with her himself (that was the kind of coward he is) knowing that it was his fault in the first place. It wasn't until he heard his name being mentioned when he stopped to listen to the rest of the argument between Stacey and Ethel, after hearing all that he needed to hear he went back into the living room and shut the door behind him.

Back in the kitchen, Ethel was still laying into Stacey and Stacey giving as good as she got, she said something to Stacey making her feel insulted and that was…

"Your grandfather should not have told you to cook our chicken the way you do yours because he doesn't even know how I like my done so therefore he must eat it because I will not be eating the chicken."

Guess what! Needless to say, the old battalacs ate the chicken that Stacey had cooked for them; I guess her stomach couldn't resist the temptation.

Feeling like we were unable to do anything for fear of breaking Ethel's ornaments which was clearly precious to her, maybe it was nerves but between myself and Tori, we accidentally broke a couple of Ethel's ornaments but the way the her things are situated, it being such small bungalow and hard to move around from room to room, something was bound to happen that is how Ethel's vase broke. One day Raymond was coming out of the kitchen with his two walking sticks, the vase was right next to the kitchen and it being a narrow doorway when Tori was backing up to let him get past her, not realising that she was too close to the vase, it fell and broke when Ethel had come out of the room (that we were sleeping in after snooping around in our things), she almost had an heart attack (literally) even though Tori apologised for what had happened and Raymond explaining that it wasn't her fault, it made no difference to Ethel all she could see was her precious vase on the floor in pieces. Ethel's first reaction was anger then she went completely quiet and locked herself in her bedroom for at least a week (the best peaceful week we ever had), but there was nothing that we could do other than buying back the vase.

Many days went by where the household became unbearable until it got to the point where Tori, Dominique, Stacey and I just barricaded ourselves in the bedroom that we were occupying and cry, we even had nights where we would cry ourselves to sleep because we were so unhappy with everything, the constant arguing between Ethel and Raymond (history repeating itself) or one of us four and that would be the time when Raymond would join in against us which was an everyday occurrence that drove all of us crazy. We could not understand what someone had to be so angry about to make them argue more than normal. Literally, from sun up to sun down, Ethel would be complaining about something or the other and when she wasn't complaining, she would be arguing.

It was the longest and excruciating 3 months of our lives all Tori, Dominique, Stacey and I did was work, work and more work day and night we would be out in the garden or out on the front lawn cutting the grass, planting her flowers, vacuuming, dusting, watering her plants, washing her windows, washing both her and her husband's dirty dishes even after we got back to the house from a long day at the library while they watched television. We would also run various errands for them such as picking up their prescription from the doctors, picking up their medicine the chemist, paying for their over due library books (which none of them know about because we did not want to brag about it), post letters for them. e.t.c you name it, we did it all for them but the ironic things about it all is that Ethel claimed we never did any house work apart from washing a few dishes, when we heard that, my daughters and I were so stunned by the fact that she would lie so blatantly.

We made sure that even though we were running all these errands for them, we would still have time for ourselves to go to the library to get out of her and

her husband's way, that was the only time my daughters and I would get any peace and when we would go out Ethel would always go into the room that we were occupying and snoop around in our belongings.

No matter what we did, Ethel was never happy which made it a lose, lose situation for my daughters and I.

Everything about that place was a nightmare, Ethel made our stay there very miserable because of her constant nagging, it would range from the bathroom routine to the domestics, going out or staying in, dinnertime, eating, whatever she fancied complaining about that day she would and the horrible part about it was, Ethel always did it well.

To make matters worse, my daughters and I already feeling like failures because of the situation that we were in, it didn't help when Ethel had her favourite grandchildren round, she would sit there rubbing their successes in our faces making my children feel even more inadequate about themselves.

"The other grandchildren has not one but two parents who is able to splash out money on their kids for various reasons even for a great education, me, I could not do that for my kids because I am the only parent that they have and always had, I just couldn't afford it, but this is something that I wouldn't bother mentioning to her because she would never understand it is almost like the others were born with a silver spoon in their mouths." This is what was going through my mind when Ethel would make her snide comments regarding myself and three daughters just to belittle us thinking that my girls do not have an education when they are clearly more intelligent than her other grandchildren.

"How can she call herself a grandmother and be so nasty to her grandchildren, if she loved them like she keeps saying she does, it wouldn't matter what situation they are in, she would love them regardless."

That's how I know Ethel never really loved me or my daughters besides it was the boys who are like the kings of the family because they are loved so much and it is always a bonus is they are educated, apart from Raymond, he was doing what he always did best and that was hiding away in the shadows, the girls are also loved even though it is in a proud way but again a bonus if they too are educated. My daughters and I are also educated; the difference is they just live different lives to the others i.e. they were born out of wedlock whereas their cousins were (all of them follow the pack but my girls are different, they have other dreams, goals and ideas in life) amongst other things that my daughters are and they aren't which is why they are automatically the black sheep of the family compared to the other grandchildren and so because of that, their cousins have started to think that they are more superior to my girls.

I always thanked God for my daughters, for their personalities, ambitions and drive that they have, no matter what disappointment life has thrown at them (and it has been a hell of a lot); they always feel the need to keep going regardless of how the rest of the family sees them.

The constant whispering had become a regular habit where Ethel and her children were concerned when they came to visit, but when they left Ethel would turn to her husband and start whispering about us to him, it would go as far as whispering about us while we were still in the same room. One day when Stacey and I was cooking our dinner, Stacey turned around to do something and that was when she caught Ethel whispering to her husband about us, pretending that she never saw anything, Stacey turned around and continued with what she was doing. On another occasion Paul came round to the house to talk to me about our living situation and to help us with a problem that we were having concerning our previous property, Ethel was sitting in the kitchen and again she felt the need to make snide remarks she said... "I want to say something but some people are narrow minded." I knew that she was calling me narrow minded and so she kept on repeating herself, I realised that she was itching to talk about me so I left the conservatory where I was sitting, to go into the bedroom, as soon as I left Ethel started whispering about me to Paul, not realising that Stacey came in (the way the house is, you would have to walk through the conservatory in the kitchen and then in the corridor to get to the bedroom), she heard Ethel talking about me to Paul even though she was trying to disguise the fact that she was doing it. I knew that whatever Ethel told Paul about me that would change his opinion of me so I decided that I no longer wanted his help.

Chapter 14

The way both Ethel and Raymond behaved those past three months while we were staying there, my daughters and I were in total shock and disbelief, to see them for who they really are, it was not a memory we will be cherishing, it is like they were not my parents.

After all these years Raymond's true colours finally came out and I can honestly say that for whatever reason, this man really despises me, he cannot stand to be around me or my children. With everything that was going on, I needed to talk to someone, but I couldn't find no one who was willing to listen to my problems, I couldn't go to anyone related to them because it would not be from an objective prospective so my daughters and I had to deal with the sufferings that Ethel and her husband was dishing out.

It reached a point where we got caught up in this petty situation where we would have an argument and it could then turn into a race for that person to tell their side of the story first, I had to because whenever Ethel told her side to her children, she would distort the whole thing and make it look like I was the bad guy so Tori, Dominique, Stacey and I made sure that we got in there first so that the story wouldn't be distorted that is what Ethel didn't like.

One day Ethel was having one of her turns when Patty walked in (all her children has her front door key which she gave them so they can walk in whenever they want to, but me, I have to knock on the door just like everyone else) Tori, Dominique, Stacey and I were in the bedroom so she didn't know that we were in there. Patty went straight into the kitchen where Ethel and Raymond were to see how they were doing, they were in the kitchen for quite a while but as Patty was leaving we over heard her say to her mum...

"Don't let them know that you have changed towards them because that's what I am doing." My children and I were wondering what could Ethel have possibly said to make Patty say such a thing when they both know that we have done nothing to them, so I decided to go and confront Patty, leaving the room I was ready to say what was on my mind but the minute Patty saw me, she ran into the kitchen and shut the door in my face.

It was bad enough that they didn't think much of us already but I knew that after this, they were going to think even less of us now that we were homeless.

"How did Vanessa manage to put the girls through this, she has ruined their lives," something that they'd say not really concerned for my girls but a way to keep reminding me what a bad mother I made. Looking down and scorning homeless people, Ethel threw away the nightclothes that we had slept in regardless of the fact that it was just a couple of days before, we had washed and didn't use them, there was a blouse that she gave me that I never wore but she threw out anyway without asking me if I had worn the blouse or not.

There were many, many arguments in the house due to Ethel's constant bad moods, one minute she was ok then the next, she would fly off the handle it was almost as if she suffered with bi-polar, but the argument that had triumphed all arguments was the one that we had on the Tuesday night, like always Ethel was in her bad mood, my daughters and I were in the bedroom as usual because we wanted to keep out of her way which didn't make a difference because Ethel came to the bedroom door shouting and screaming at us for something that we apparently done or didn't do (I don't know), I tried to talk to her but realised that I was not getting through to her she was just ranting and raving it got so bad that Tori burst out crying then she ran out of the house to see if she could get any help from Patrick who lives approximately four doors away, with Stacey right behind her and no shoes on her feet. Ringing the doorbell to see if she could get an answer Tori was hysterical, when Patrick's wife eventually opened the door, she asked Stacey and Tori what was wrong and because Tori was unable to answer, Stacey had to explain what was going on back at the house, she told her that myself and Ethel were arguing and Ethel was throwing us out. After hearing all of this, Patrick's wife said that she was going to get her shoes and coat and see what was going on, trying not to disturb Patrick who was ill at the time but when he heard, he asked what was happening so Stacey had to explain to him, again after hearing the situation, Patrick decided to come along to see if he could solve the problem.

When Stacey and Tori got back to the house with Patrick and his wife behind them, Ethel and I were still arguing, this time, old feelings came up and one of them was that she took my daughters toys when they were younger and handed them out to the rest of the family, Dominique was so hurt that she was the one who reminded Ethel of what she had done but with no surprise, Ethel had denied the whole thing with Raymond backing her up. As time was getting later and it was approaching 11:00pm, my daughters and I were packing our belongings with Ethel in our ears saying...

"Get out of my house, please pack faster I can't wait until your house comes through because I want you out of mine."

Standing there shocked by his mother's and father's behaviour, Patrick could do nothing to solve the problem, exactly at 11:00pm, my daughters and I were thrown unto the streets by Ethel and Raymond closing the door behind them so we left out in the freezing cold to find some where to stay. While we were out in the cold, someone came up to us and offered us a place to stay with him and his friends for the night he asked why we were out in the cold so late at night and my response was...

"I just had an argument with my mother and her and her husband threw us out."

His response to that was... "She is so wicked to do that to her daughter and grandchildren."

So we went with the guy to the place where he said that we could stay the night and that's where we slept.

The next day I received a phone call from Melvin saying that he heard what had happened the previous night and that he was going to call a family meeting to solve the issue, I was apprehensive for many reasons but then I decided to hear what he had to say on the matter. The meeting started at 8:00pm Patty, Melvin, Patrick, my daughters and I all went back to the house to try and sort things out. Ethel said her piece, I said my piece and my daughters said their piece, needless to say that everything we said, Ethel denied, time was swiftly moving on, it was getting late and knowing that we were not achieving anything, Melvin decided to call it a day. When we left the house, I told Melvin that I was disowning these two people and he said that him and Patrick was going to sort things out between us and the rest of the family but they were going to wait until we got back on our feet, but I can safely say that it will not be happening because Dominique, Tori, Stacey and I

just aren't interested any more in patching things up with anyone, we have given them years of chances when some people would say that we were stupid to keep putting ourselves back in the firing line, forgiving them countless times, we feel that it is not worth it anymore. As far as I was concerned, Ethel and Raymond were no longer my parents, I could not look either one of them in the eyes anymore and see pure hate, after all these years my daughters and I just couldn't take feeling inadequate around them.

Since that night my daughters and I have not spoke to either of them. No one In that family understands how we feel or felt, my daughters and I never had a decent life because of Ethel and her family and also people who called themselves friends, it didn't help with the way our lives taking such a drastic turn for the worse, no one stopped to think how all this affected my children and I. Cutting ourselves from the family emotionally is the best thing that we have ever done, knowing that we were not getting anywhere with them despite everything that I have been through all the emotional, physical and mental abuse that I had to suffer at the hands of that woman who was suppose to be a loving and nurturing, having children of my own, experiencing life with them, I believe that as long as you have breath it's never too late to start over, and realising that wonderful things can still happen.

It took us a while to believe in ourselves, to realise that our problems can either make or break us, but my daughters and I can say that our situation has made us who we are today which is stronger, more determined to achieve our goals in life and not let anyone stand in our way if they are not beneficial to our growth. Grabbing life with both hands and constantly trying new things that are when we will discover what life really has to offer and great things are out there for everyone no matter what our status is in life.

As a single mother to three children who I am extremely proud of, the strong and independent young women that they have turned out to be and not allowing the pressures and disappointments of life to hold them back, going for their dreams and living life, after all life is there to be lived...

So live it.

THE END